THE
MASTER MIND

THE
MASTER MIND

by Theron Q. Dumont

The Unparalleled Classic on
Wielding Your Mental Powers
From the Author of
The Kybalion

Abridged and Introduced
by Mitch Horowitz

THE CONDENSED 📖 CLASSICS LIBRARY™

MEDIA

Published by Gildan Media LLC
aka G&D Media.
www.GandDmedia.com

The Master Mind was originally published in 1918
G&D Media Condensed Classics edition published 2018
Abridgement and Introduction copyright © 2017 by Mitch
Horowitz

FIRST EDITION: 2018

Cover design by David Rheinhardt of Pyrographx

Interior design by Meghan Day Healey of Story Horse, LLC.

ISBN: 978-1-7225-0062-7

CONTENTS

The Enduring Genius
of *The Master Mind*

This is a distinctly different kind of book to come from the author who used the pseudonymous byline "Theron Q. Dumont." The man behind this penetrating, practical work of psychology was William Walker Atkinson, a prolific writer and publisher of New Thought and metaphysical literature in the early-twentieth century. Atkinson's most successful and influential work was the 1908 occult classic, *The Kybalion*, which he also wrote pseudonymously under the mysterious byline "Three Initiates."

Yet this work, *The Master Mind*, published ten years later, is notable for its absence of any mystical content. For a man who intensively studied the spiritual ideas of

New Thought—or what William James called "the religion of healthy-mindedness"—this book represented a sharp departure. *The Master Mind* is probably Atkinson's most straightforward work of psychology. In fact, the book's great value is that it may be the best popularization ever of the psychological and self-development ideas of William James. James, like Atkinson, believed in the ability of the individual to harness and direct the practical faculties of his mind. A person's failure to use his mental forces, James reasoned, regulated him to a random and automatized existence, in which covert motives and desires shoved and shuffled him around.

The chief aim of this book is to teach you to become aware of and command your mental and emotional faculties. The book's techniques are drawn from the work of James and other practical psychologists of the era, whose ideas have proven remarkably resilient and, in many ways, remain as radical today as they were in the early part of the last century. The continued urgency of these methods is due not only to their truthfulness, but also to their persistent neglect. People typically acknowledge but fail to attempt most techniques of inner development. Hence, much of the material in *The Master Mind* awaits rediscovery and full use by the intrepid reader.

Another philosophical correspondence, if not influence, found in this book is between Atkinson's ideas and those of early-twentieth century spiritual teacher G.I. Gurdjieff. The Russian mystic and philosopher, more than any other figure of the last century, described man's state of automatism and his alienation from the forces, interior and exterior, that rule his life. Atkinson's analysis of the individual as an ineptly steered chariot in chapter four corresponds remarkably well with Gurdjieff's metaphor of an unruly horse-and-carriage representing man's disordered state. Atkinson also shares, to some degree, Gurdjeff's identification of a lost but central "I" within the individual.

Although Atkinson's death in 1932 made him contemporaneous to Gurdjieff, it is not clear to me that he ever actually encountered the teacher's ideas—I have come across no such reference in his work. But some of Atkinson's coinciding insights demonstrate just how insightful the writer-publisher was to evince points of commonality with the vitally important esoteric philosopher Gurdjieff.

Some observers have made the mistake—and I was once among them—of underestimating Atkinson as a thinker due to his frequent use of dramatic-sounding bylines and covert identities. Today, however, Atkinson is rightly becoming recognized not only for the breadth of his output, but also for the sturdiness of his ideas. I believe that within a generation Atkinson will be recognized as one of the two or three brightest and most literate voices to emerge from the New Thought tradition. Another is the mystic Neville Goddard, whose work emerged in the generation following Atkinson's.

In this condensed book, I have endeavored to preserve Atkinson's shrewdest insights into human nature, and his most practical and doable exercises for mental and emotional self-development. All of these exercises are canny and realistic. There is no excuse for not doing them. The long-term payoff, Atkinson promised, is honing your command over the instrumentalities of your thought, emotions, and willpower—which will result in the development of a Master Mind, and a true sense of selfhood. It is an epic promise, and one worthy of striving toward.

Finally, in this abridgment, I have identified the philosophers and psychologists that Atkinson quotes, who he sometimes referenced only generally and not by name in his original edition. I have also omitted quotation marks and attributions from passages where Atkinson quotes his own writing as published under a different byline.

This new edition of *The Master Mind* gives you a sense of the hope and excitement that early-twentieth century readers found in the theories of "healthy-mindedness." I think you will come to share my conviction that the book's immensely practical ideas await new discovery and use today.

—Mitch Horowitz

CHAPTER ONE

The Master Mind

In this book there will be nothing said concerning metaphysical theories or philosophical hypotheses; instead, there will be a very strict adherence to the principles of psychology. There will be nothing said of "spirit" or "soul;" but very much said of "mind." There will be no speculation concerning the question of "what is the soul?" or "what becomes of the soul after death?" These subjects, while highly important and interesting, belong to a different class of investigation, and are outside of the present inquiry. We shall not even enter into a discussion of the subject of "what is the mind?" Instead, we shall confine our thought to the subject of "how does the mind work?"

Many philosophers and metaphysicians have sought to tell us "just what" the mind is; but they usually leave us as much in doubt as before. As the old Persian poet has said, we "come out the door in which we went." We know much about **how the mind works**, but little or nothing about **what the mind really is**. So far as practical purposes are concerned, it makes very little difference to us just what the mind **is**, providing we know just how it **works**, and how it may be controlled and managed.

We shall operate according to the principle of pragmatism, as described by William James: "Pragmatism is the attitude of looking away from first things, principles, categories, supposed necessities; and of looking forward toward last things, fruits, consequences, facts."

What is the difference between a Master Mind and any other form of Mind? Simply that the Master Mind is consciously, deliberately, and voluntarily built up, cultivated, developed, and used; whereas the ordinary mind is usually unconsciously built up, cultivated, and developed, without voluntary effort on its own part, but solely by the force and power of impressions from the outside world, and is usually employed and used with little or no conscious direction by its own will.

In short, the ordinary mind is a mere creature of circumstances, driven by the winds of outside forces, and lacking the guidance of the hand on the wheel, and without the compass of knowledge; while the Master Mind proceeds in the true course mapped out by Intelligence, and determined by will—with sails set so as to catch the best breeze from the outside world, and steered by the master-hand at the wheel, under the direction of the compass of intelligence. The ordinary mind is like a dumb, driven animal; while the Master Mind is like the strong-willed, intelligent, masterful Man.

We can deliberately and voluntarily select and choose the particular wind which is to force our mental boat forward or, changing the figure, to choose and select the particular stream of thought and feeling which is to be allowed to flow through our mind.

There are three general conditions of human mentality: (1) Mental Slavery, in which the mind is the slave and servant of outside forces and influences; (2) Partial Freedom, in which the mind is largely controlled by outside influences, while at the same time a limited amount of voluntary control and direction has been acquired; and (3) Mental Mastery, in which the mental faculties, and emotional organism, have been brought under the control of the will and judgment, and the individual is a master of, and not a slave to, environment and circumstances. The great masses of people are in the first class; a comparatively small number have passed into the second; while a still smaller number have passed into the third class, and have become the Master Minds of their time and place.

We moderns are unaccustomed to the mastery over our inner thoughts and feelings. That a man should fall prey to any thought that happens to take possession of his mind is commonly assumed as unavoidable. It may be a matter of regret that he should be kept awake all night from anxiety, and that he should have the power of determining whether he be kept awake seems an extravagant demand. The image of an impending calamity is no doubt odious, but its very odiousness (we say) makes it haunt the mind all the more pertinaciously, and it is useless to expel it. Yet this is an absurd position for man, the heir of all the ages, to be lag-ridden by the flimsy creatures of his own brain. If a pebble in our boot torments us, we expel it. We take off the boot and shake it out. And once the matter is fairly understood, it is just as easy to expel an intruding and obnoxious thought. It *should* be as easy to expel an obnoxious thought from the mind as to shake a stone out of your shoe; and until a man can do that, it is nonsense to talk about his ascendancy over nature. He is a mere slave, and a prey to the bat-winged phantoms that flit through the corridors of his own brain.

It is one of the prominent doctrines of some of the Eastern schools of practical psychology that the power of expelling thoughts, or if need be, killing them dead on the spot, **must** be attained. Naturally the art requires practice; but, like other arts, when once acquired there is no mystery or difficulty about it. It is *worth practice*. It may be fairly said that life only begins when this art has been acquired. For obviously when, instead of being ruled by individual thoughts, the whole flock of them in their immense multitude, variety, and capacity is ours to direct, dispatch, and employ where we will, life becomes so vast and grand, compared to what it was before, that its former condition may well appear almost ante-natal. If you can kill a thought dead, for the time being, you can do anything else with it that you please. And therefore is this power so valuable. It not only frees a man from mental torment (which is at least nine-tenths the torment of life), but it also gives him a concentrated power of handling mental work absolutely unknown to him before.

Another facet of the Master Mind is that while at work your thought is absolutely concentrated upon and in it, undistracted by anything whatever irrelevant to the matter in hand. Then when the work is finished, if there is no more occasion for the use of the machine, it stops equally, absolutely, and entirely—with no **worrying**—and the man retires into that region of his consciousness where his true self dwells. The power of the thought-machine is enormously increased by this faculty of letting it alone on the one hand, and of using it singly and with concentration on the other.

The subjection of thought is closely related to the subjection of desire, and consequently has especially moral as well as especially intellectual relation to the question in hand. Nine-tenths of the scattered or sporadic thought with which the mind occupies itself, when not concentrated on any definite work, is what may be called s*elf-thought*—thought which dwells on and exaggerates the sense of self. This is hardly realized in its full degree until the effort is made to suppress it; and one of the most excellent results of such an effort is that with the stilling of all the phantoms which hover around the lower self, one's relations to others, to one's friends, to the world at large, and one's perceptions of all that is concerned in these relations, come out into a purity and distinctness unknown before. Obviously, when the mind is full of little desires and fears, which concern the local self, and is clouded over by the thought images, which such desires and fears evoke, it is impossible that it should see and understand the greater facts beyond, and its own relation to them. But with the subsiding of the former, the great vision begins to dawn; and a man never feels less alone than when he has ceased to think whether he is alone.

The Master Mind creates a world for itself, in which it dwells supreme, and to which it attracts and draws what is conducive to its welfare and happiness, its success and achievement.

You are invited to become a Master Mind. Will you accept the invitation? If so, you will carefully study the principles herein explained, and apply the methods described.

Chapter Two

The Mind Master

The idea of "mastery" carries with it the notion of dominion, power, or supremacy exercised by some person or thing, which is regarded as the "master." The spirit and essence of the term "master" is that of governor, ruler, director, leader, manager, or controller.

Some psychologists would have us believe that the intellectual faculties are the governing powers of the mind. But it will take but little thought to inform us that in many cases the intellectual powers are not the masterful forces in the mental activities of the individual; in many cases the feelings, desires, and emotional factors of the person run away with his reason, and not only cause him to do things that his reason tells him he should not, but also so influence his reason that his "reasons" are usually merely excuses for his actions performed in response to feelings and emotions.

Other psychologists would have us believe that the desires, feelings, and emotions of the individual are his mental masters; and in many cases it would appear that this is true, for many persons allow their feelings, emotions, and passions to govern them almost entirely, all else being subordinated to these. But when we begin to examine closely into the matter we find that in the case of certain individuals there is a greater or lesser subordination of the feelings and emotions to the dictates of reason; and in the case of persons of excellent self-control, the reason would appear to be higher in authority than the feelings. In the case of recognized Mental Masters, it is even found that the very feelings, passions, and emotions are so obedient to higher mental authority that in many cases they may actually be transformed and transmuted into other forms of feeling and emotion in response to the orders or commands of the central authority.

The thoughtful investigator usually discovers that the Mind Master is not found in the respective realms of the first two of the three great divisions of the mental kingdom, i.e., in the division of Thought, or that of Feeling, respectively. The investigator then turns to the third great division of the mental kingdom, i.e., that of Will, in his search for the sovereign power. And at first, it would appear that here, in the region of the Will, he had found the object of his search; and that the Will must be acclaimed the master. But when the matter is gone into a little deeper, the investigator discovers that not in Will itself, but in a *Something* lying at the very center of Will, is found the Mind Master.

While it is seen that the Will is higher in power and authority than either Thought or Feeling, it is also seen by the careful investigator that, in most cases, the Will is controlled and brought into activity by the Feelings; and that in other cases, it is started into action by the result of Thought, or intellectual effort. This being so, the Will cannot be considered as being always the Mind Master. And, discovering this, the investigator at first begins to feel discouraged, and to imagine that he is but traveling around a circle; in fact, many thinkers would have us believe that the mental processes work around in a circle, and that like a ring the process has no point of beginning or ending. But those who have persisted in the search have been rewarded by a higher discovery. They have found that while many persons are impelled to will by reason of their feelings and emotions, and others by reason of their thoughts, there is a third class of individuals—a smaller class to be sure—who seem to be masters of the will-activity, and who, standing in the position of a judge and sovereign power, first care- fully weigh the merits of both feelings and thoughts, and then decide to exercise the willpower in a certain determined direction. This last class of individuals may be said to really *will to will* by the exercise of some higher authority within them. These are the real Master Minds. Let us seek to discover the secret of their power.

THE CENTRAL AUTHORITY

There is in the mental realm of every individual a certain *Something* that occupies the position of Central Authority, Power, and Control over the entire mental kingdom of that person. In many case —in **most** cases, we regret to say—this *Something* seems to be asleep, and the kingdom is allowed to run itself, "higgledy-piggledy," automatically and like a piece of senseless machinery, or else under the control of outside mentalities and personalities. In other cases—in **many** cases, in fact—this Central Authority has partially awakened, and consequently exerts at least a measure of its authority over its kingdom, but at the same time fails to realize its full powers, or to exert its full authority; it acts like a man only half-awakened from his sleep, and still in a state of partial doze.

Rising in the scale, we find cases of still greater degree of "awakening," until finally we discover the third great class of individuals—a very small class!— in whom the Central Authority has become almost or quite fully awake; and in whom this Mind Master has taken active control of his kingdom, and has begun to assert his authority and power over it.

You, the person now reading these words—YOU, yourself—are now asked to make this search of your mental kingdom, this search that has for its aim the discovery of the *Something Within* yourself that is the Mind Master, and which, when fully aroused into conscious power and activity, makes you a Master Mind.

All "voluntary attention" is performed by the exercise of this power of the will, exerted by this *Something Within* that we call "I," and which proves itself to be the Master of Thoughts.

The individual who has trained his mind to obey his will, is able to direct his thought processes just as he directs his feet, hands, or body, or just as he guides and manages his team of horses or his car. This being so, we cannot consider our Thought processes or faculties as the Mind Master; but must look for the Master in something still higher in authority.

There seems to be but one other region of the mind in which to search for our Mind Master, or Central Authority. You naturally say here, "He means The Will." But is it merely the Will? Stop a moment and consider. If the Will, in itself, is the Mind Master, why is it that the Will, in the case of so many persons, allows itself to be controlled and called into action by ordinary feelings, desires, emotions, or passions, or on the other hand is called into action by the most trifling, passing thought or idea? In such cases it appears that the Will is really the obedient, "easy" servant, rather than the Master.

That the machinery of the Will is the mechanism of control and action, is undoubted; but what is it that controls and directs the Will in the cases of individuals of strong Willpower? In such cases it would seem that not only must the Will be strong, but there must be some stronger *Something* that is able to control, direct, and apply the power of the Will. In moments in which you have exerted your Willpower, did you identify yourself with your Will, or did you feel that your Will was an instrument of power "belonging to" you, and being operated by you? Were you not at such moments aware of feeling an overwhelming consciousness of the existence of your **self**, or "I," at the center of your mental being? And of feeling that, at least for the time, this "I" was the Master of all the rest of your mental equipment? We think that you will agree to this statement, if you will carefully live over again the experiences of such moments, and in imagination and memory reenact the experience.

All mental analysis brings the individual to the realization that at the very center of his mental being there dwells a *Something*—and he always calls this "I"— which is the **permanent** element of his being. While his sensations, feelings, emotions, tastes, thoughts, beliefs, ideas, and even ideals have changed from time to time, he knows to a certainty that this "I" has been permanent, and that it is the same old "I" that has always been present throughout his life, from his earliest days. He knows that although his emotional nature, and general mental-physical character may have undergone an almost total transformation, this "I" has never really changed at all, but has ever remained "the same I."

Moreover, while the individual may change his sensations, feelings, tastes, passions, emotions, and whole general character in some cases, he is never able to change in the slightest degree this *Something Within* that he calls "I." He can never run away from this "I," nor can he ever move it from its position. He can never lift his "I" by means of his mental bootstraps; nor can his personal shadow run away from this "I" of his individuality. He may set apart for consideration each and every one of his mental experiences, sensations, thoughts, feelings, ideas, and all the rest; but he can never set off from himself this "I" for such inspection. He can know this "I" only as his self, that *Something Within* at the very center of his consciousness.

We are conscious of something closer to the center than anything else. Sensations originate outside and inside of the body. Emotions originate inside of the body. But this *Something* is deeper than either, and both are objective to it. We cannot classify it with anything else. We cannot describe it in terms of any other form of consciousness. Other forms of consciousness are objective in their relation to it, but it is never objective to them. There is nothing in our consciousness deeper. It underlies and overlies and permeates all other forms, and, moreover,—what is of immeasurably greater importance—it can, if need be, create them.

Just what this "I" is, we cannot tell. This riddle has never been solved by the reason of man. So subtle is its essence that it is almost impossible to think of it as a something apart from its mental states. All that can be said of it is that *it is*. Its only report of itself is "I Am."

This *Something Within*—this "I"—is that entity in philosophy and metaphysics that has been called "The Ego;" but such name does nothing in the way of defining it. You need not speculate over just what the Ego is, for you will never learn this. All that you can know is that it IS.

Your task is not to try to learn what the Ego is, for as has been said, you will never know this. Your task is to strive to awaken it into active consciousness, so that it may realize its power, and begin to employ it. You can awaken it by the proper mental attitude—by the conscious realization of its presence and power. And you can gradually cause it to realize its power, and to use it, by means of exercises calling into play that power. This is what Willpower really means. Your Will is strong already—it does not need strengthening; what is needed is that you urge your Ego into realizing that it can use your Willpower. You must learn to gradually awaken the half-asleep Giant, and set it to work in its own natural field of endeavor.

He who will carefully consider the above statements, and will make them a part of his mental armament, will have grasped the secret of the Master Mind.

Chapter Three

The Slave Will
and The Master Will

The masses of people are really little more than automatons. Their wills are called into activity by every passing desire, their passions and desires are uncontrolled, and their thought-processes are the result of suggestions made by others, which they accept and then fondly imagine they have thought for themselves.

The wills of such persons are Slave Wills, subject to the influence, control, and direction of others. The will-processes of such persons are almost entirely what are known as "reflex" activities, requiring the employment of but little powers of judgment, and little or no exercise of voluntary control.

Some may object that we are making too strong a statement when we say that the mental activity of the great masses of people are practically akin to reflex actions. People "think" about what they do before doing it, these objectors say. Of course "people think;" or, rather, they "think that they think;" but in reality the process of their "thinking" is almost reflex, that is to say it is automatic and mechanical, rather than deliberate. Their thought is usually based upon some suggested premise—some so-called fact accepted through suggestion and without verification or real consideration. Their accepted "facts" are usually found to agree with their likes, feelings, or prejudices, rather than based upon careful investigation. Their so-called "reasons" are but excuses or explanations evolved to justify their decision or action, both of these really based upon desires, wishes, likes, or prejudices.

Practically all our voluntary acts of will result from the power of **desire**. But this does not imply, by any means, that **all** desires result in action. The rule is this: **The greater the degree of the willpower of the individual, the greater is his degree of control over his desires**. And, as we have seen that the degree of willpower is the degree of the "wakefulness" of the Ego, it follows that **the greater the wakefulness of the Ego,**

the greater the degree of its control over the desires found within its mental realm.

Every human being is, from the cradle to the grave, subject to external restraint. If a man declares that he is free to go without food, air, and sleep, and tries to act accordingly, consequences will soon deprive him of that liberty. The circle of freedom is much smaller than is sometimes thought; the fish is never free to become an eagle. Human freedom may be likened to a vessel sailing—freedom consists in being able to choose between two or more alternative courses of action.

The average man will indignantly deny that his freedom of will-action is in any way affected or restricted by outside or inside influences. He says triumphantly: "**I can act as I wish,**" thinking that he has answered the argument against free will. But here is the point: he can act **only** as he **wishes**; and if his **wishes** are controlled or determined in any way, then so are his actions controlled and determined. And as his "wishes" are but forms of his **desires**, then unless he controls his desires he does not control his wishes, but is controlled by them. And as the average man has not acquired a strong control of his desires, he is lacking to that extent in his freedom of will-action. And right here is the main distinction between the Slave Will and the Master Will.

The Slave Will obeys the orders of its desires, feelings, and other "wishes," the latter coming from Lord-knows-where into his mental field. Such a man is not free, in the true sense of the word. He is a slave to his wishes, feelings, desires, passions—and he has no control over the thoughts and ideas that feed these desires, and that often actually **create** them. The Master Will not only refuses to he controlled by the intruding desires, if these are deemed against his best interests, but he actually controls them—by controlling the ideas and thoughts that serve to feed and nourish these desires, and in many cases, have also created them.

Our world is very much what we choose to pay attention to.

Ideas detained in consciousness tend to fan the flame of feeling; these ideas may be dismissed and others summoned to repress the flame of feeling. **In the higher type of action, the will can go out only in the direction of an idea. Every idea that becomes an object of desire is a motive**. It is true that the will tends to go out in the direction of the greatest motive, that is, toward the object that seems the most desirable; but the will, through voluntary attention, puts energy into a motive idea and thus makes it strong. It is impossible to center the attention long on an idea without developing positive or negative interest, attraction or repulsion.

Thus does the will develop motives. We may state it as a law that **the will determines which motives shall become the strongest, by determining which ideas shall occupy the field of consciousness.**

If one idea is kept before the mind, a desire and a strong motive may gather around that idea. If another idea is called in, the power of the first idea will decline. Voluntary attention makes the motive. The motive does not make the attention. Hence, the motive is a product of the will. If I withdraw my attention from a motive idea, it loses vigor. The only way to develop and maintain a free will is to direct the attention and thought by means of the awakened Ego—the Master Mind and Mind Master.

Chapter Four

Positive and Negative Mentality

There is always a "two-sidedness" in individuals. Every individual finds within a constant struggle between these two opposing elements—the positive and the negative. Upon the outcome of this battle depends largely the advancement, success, welfare, and progress of the individual. Goethe has said: "In my breast, alas, two souls dwell, all there is unrest. Each with the other strives for mastery, each from the other struggles to be free." The ordinary individual seems content to remain a passive spectator of this struggle; but the individual of the awakened Ego takes part in the struggle, and by throwing the weight of his freewill into the balance, he brings down the scales on the positive side.

When the individual is forced to consider any feeling, emotion, idea, action, advice, suggestion, or teaching, he should always submit it to the Touchstone of Positivity, by asking himself: **"Will this make me stronger, more powerful, more capable, more efficient, better?"** It becomes the duty of every individual wishing to progress on the Path of Life, and desiring to become proficient and capable in his expression and manifestation of mentality and character, to cultivate the positive qualities of the mind, and to restrain and inhibit the negative ones. In the consideration of this matter you should always remember that every positive quality has its negative opposite. This is an invariable rule, and one that you may test for yourself. And arising from it is this important rule of the new psychology: "To develop a positive quality, you should restrain or inhibit its opposing negative: To restrain or inhibit a negative quality, you should develop and encourage its opposing positive."

Man should be more than a mere creature of chance, environment, and outside influences. He should be ruled from within—be self-ruled—instead of being merely a weak instrument of desire, emotion, and feeling, influenced by suggestions and impressions from every passing person or thing. Man should be directed and guided by the strong instrument of his will, held firmly to its task by the Ego.

The fundamental idea of the new psychology is embodied in the symbol of the charioteer driving his fiery steeds under full control and with taut rein. The chariot represents the being of the man; the charioteer, the Ego; the reins, the will; the steeds, the mental states of feeling, emotion, desire, imagination, and the rest. Unless the reins be strong, they will not be sufficient to control the horses. Unless the charioteer be trained and vigilant, the horses will run away with the chariot and dash to pieces the driver in the general wreck. But controlled and mastered, the fiery steeds will lead forward to attainment and accomplishment, and at the same time will travel the road in safety.

There comes a time in the life of each one of us when the following question must be answered, and your course chosen. It may be that this time has come to you in the reading of these lines. Are you ready to answer it, and to make the decision? Remember the question. It is this: "Mastery or Servitude—Which?"

A man grows to resemble his ideals. And a man's ideals are the outgrowth of his feelings and emotions. The ideal held by the man arouses interest in all things connected with it. Interest is the strong motive of attention; and attention is the beginning of all the activities of the will. So the man's ideals serve to set into activity the chain of mental cause and effect that results in storing away in his mind the strong impressions that have so much to do with the building up of character. A man tends to grow to resemble the things he likes, and in which he is interested.

So true is this that a writer has suggested that we say, "As a man loveth, so is he." But here again the Master Mind asserts its power, and says: "I love that which I want to love—I am free here as in all else in my realm."

Modern psychology teaches us that the two following principles are operative in the character of each individual: (1) That feelings manifest themselves in will-action, unless inhibited or controlled; and (2) that the will-action follows the lines of the strongest interest.

We constantly act, often unconsciously, in accordance with our strongest desires, feelings, likes or dislikes, prejudices, etc. The Master Mind recognizes this and places in that storehouse only what he chooses to go into it, and what he chooses to come out of it as the incentive to action—being always governed in his choice by the Rule of Positivity heretofore announced: **"Will this make me stronger, more powerful, more capable, more efficient, better?"**

To many people the suggestion that they have the **power** to select the objects of their interest may seem absurd. They are accustomed to regard interest, feelings, desires, emotions, and even passions, as things beyond their control, so that they make no attempt to exercise a voluntary control over them. It is true that these mental states do not spring from pure intellectual effort—they spring from the depths of the subconscious mentality, unbidden, in most cases. But the facts of the new psychology show us plainly that the Ego may assume control of these involuntary mental states, and either encourage and develop them, or else restrain or inhibit them entirely. Just as the will may assume control of certain muscles of the body, so may the Ego assume control of the entire mental kingdom, and mold, build, change, and improve each and every department of its mental workshop. Interest results from attention, and may be controlled by the will. **And the will is the chief instrument of the Ego.**

Chapter Five

Attention

Considering how frequently we employ the term "Attention," and its importance in our mental processes and their resulting action, it is strange how little thought we have given to the question: "What is Attention?"

Philosopher William Hamilton has said: "Attention is consciousness, and something more. It is consciousness voluntarily applied to some determinate object. **It is consciousness concentrated**."

Attention is not an enlargement or increase in consciousness, but rather a narrowing, condensing, or limiting of consciousness. The act of Attention may be said to consist of three phases: (1) The earnest **fixing** of the mind upon some particular object; (2) the persistent **holding** of the mind upon that object; and (3) the determined **shutting-out** of the mind (for the time being) the perception of any other objects struggling for conscious recognition and attention.

To paraphrase one authority: The most important intellectual habit that I know of is attending exclusively to the matter in hand. It is commonly said that genius cannot be infused by education, yet this is the power of **concentrated Attention.**

And another: The force wherewith anything strikes the mind is generally in proportion to the degree of Attention bestowed upon it. The more completely the mental energy can be brought into one focus, and all distracting objects excluded, by the act of Attention, the more powerful will be the volitional effort.

There are two phases of Attention: (1) **reflex**, and (2) **voluntary** attention. **Reflex Attention** is drawn from us by a nervous response to some stimulus. **Voluntary Attention** is given by us to some object of our own selection, and is accompanied by a peculiar sense of effort. Many persons scarcely get beyond the reflex stage. Any chance stimulus will take their attention away.

In voluntary Attention, we make a deliberate selection of the object to which we wish our mind to attend. Again, in involuntary Attention there is no sense of effort; while in voluntary Attention there is always a peculiar sense of effort, sometimes to a very marked degree.

The first step toward the development of the will lies

in the exercise of Attention. There is a sense of conscious effort in voluntary Attention. This suffices to mark it off from the involuntary type. If we take two ideas of the same intensity, and center the attention upon one, we shall notice how much it grows in power. If we, at the start, want several things in about an equal degree, whether a bicycle, a typewriter, or an encyclopedia, we shall end by wanting the one most on which our attention has been most strongly centered. Attention is the most important element in will. In order to act in the direction of one idea in preference to another, we must dismiss the one and voluntarily attend to the other. The motor force thus developed in connection with the dominant idea lies at the foundation of every higher act of will.

Psychologist Rueben Post Halleck has written: "When it is said that Attention will not take hold on an uninteresting object, we must not forget that anyone not shallow and fickle can soon discover something interesting in most objects. Here cultivated minds show their especial superiority, for the Attention that they are able to give generally finds a pearl in the most uninteresting looking oyster. When an object necessarily loses interest from one point of view, such minds discover in it new attributes. The essence of genius is to present an old thing in new ways, whether it be some force in nature or some aspect in humanity."

Chapter Six

The Mastery of Perception

Psychologist William Walter Smith has given us perhaps the most comprehensive, and at the same time the most condensed, statement of the Laws of Attention, which I paraphrase:

(1) Attention will not attach itself to uninteresting things. (2) It will soon decline in vigor (a) if the stimulus is unvarying, or (b) if some new attribute is not discovered in the object. (3) Attention cannot remain constant in the same direction for a long period, because (a) the nervous apparatus of the senses soon tire under the strain of continuous attention toward any one object, and consequently respond with less vigor, (b) the same is true of brain cells. To prove the truth of this one has only to focus the eye continuously on one object, or to keep the attention fixed on the same phase of a subject. (4) When one kind of attention is exhausted, we

may rest ourselves in two ways: (a) by giving ourselves up to the play of reflex (involuntary) attention, or (b) by directing our voluntary attention into a new channel. The amount of fatigue must determine which is better. (5) Attention too continuously centered upon the same unvarying sensation, or upon any unchanging object, has been proved by experiment to tend to induce either the hypnotic state or a comatose condition.

The first of the above laws states the difficulty of attaching the Attention to uninteresting things. But there is a remedy for this as follows: (a) in the application of the equally true principle that interest may be developed in a previously uninteresting thing by studying and analyzing it. Everything has its interesting side, and examination will bring this into view. (b) By viewing a thing from varying viewpoints, and from different angles of physical and mental vision, new facts are discovered regarding it, and these discoveries awaken interest and renewed Attention.

The same remedy applies in the case of the second law. For by changing the point of view, and by discovering new qualities, properties, and attributes in a thing, the stimulus is varied, and renewed interest is obtained.

The third law explains why the Attention cannot long remain focused in the same direction. A remedy for this will be found in the well-known psychological rule to study a thing by piecemeal. That is to say, instead of considering attentively the entire subject, or object, one should break it (mentally) into as many small sections as possible, and then proceed to study it by sections. This will vary the stimulus.

The fourth law informs us that we may obtain rest for the tired Attention by (a) relaxing the voluntary Attention, and opening our consciousness to the impressions of involuntary, or reflex Attention—paying attention to the sights and sounds reaching us from outside, as for instance by closing our book and looking out of the window at the passing persons and things; or (b) by directing our voluntary Attention into a new channel, as by closing our book and picking up and reading another book along entirely different lines; or changing from an abstract subject to a concrete proposition, or vice versa. This expresses an important psychological principle, i.e., that the best way to rest and relax the Attention is to change the direction of its effort and activity. Change of occupation gives the best kind of rest to physical or mental muscles.

The fifth law merely serves to emphasize the effect of the unnatural concentration of Attention; and the fact that a varying stimulus is necessary for continued consciousness. It serves to point us to the middle of the road, avoiding the extreme of undue concentration on a single object on the one hand, and the other extreme of bestowing no voluntary Attention at all.

The average person is able to arouse and maintain Attention only when interest already attaches to the object to be considered. But the Master Mind rides over this obstacle by first awakening interest in the thing by means of a careful examination under concentrated voluntary Attention, and thereafter allowing the Attention to flow freely along the channels of interest thus made. Here we have an instance of the will first creating a channel, and then traveling over its course.

CHAPTER SEVEN

The Mastery of Emotion

Feeling and Emotion are the great incentives to action, and the great motive-power of mental and physical manifestations. Even Intellect, that supposed monarch of the mental world, really is "under the thumb" of that "power behind the throne," which we know as Feeling and Emotion. Not only do we act according to our feelings, but in most cases we also think according to them. Instead of reasoning coldly and without prejudice, we really generally reason along the lines of our strong feelings. Instead of finding real "reasons" for our actions, we usually seek merely for "excuses" to justify our actions in accordance with our feelings.

There are few people able to detach themselves, even in a small degree, from their feelings, so as to decide questions by pure reason or intellectual effort. Moreover, there are few whose wills are guided by pure reason; their feelings supply the motive for the majority of the acts of will. The intellect, even when used, is generally employed to carry out the dictates of Feeling and Desire. Much of our reasoning is performed in order to justify our feelings, or to find proofs for the position dictated by our desires, feelings, sympathies, prejudices, or sentiments. It has been said that "men seek not reasons, but excuses, for their actions."

Our judgments are affected by our feelings. It is much easier to approve of the actions of some person whom we like, or whose views accord with our own, than of an individual whose personality and views are distasteful to us. It is very difficult to prevent prejudice, for or against anything, from influencing our judgments. It is also true that "we find that for which we look" in things and people, and that which we expect and look for is often dependent upon our feelings. If we dislike a person or thing, we usually perceive no end of undesirable qualities in him or it; while if we are favorably inclined we easily find many admirable qualities in the same person or thing. A little change in our feeling often results in the formation of an entirely new set of judgments regarding a person or thing.

The true Master Mind impresses its dominion upon the Feelings and Emotions, and then **sets them to work** in the right direction. In fact, it is by means of the powers of Feeling and Emotion that the Master

Mind accomplishes much of its work. This should be borne in mind by the reader who wishes to develop the Master Mind.

Particularly in its phase of Desire does the Master Mind make use of Feeling and Emotion. Desire may be said to be *concentrated Feeling*. Before we can have ambition or aspiration, there must be desire. Before we can manifest courage or energy, there must be desire. Desire for something must underlie all life-action—desire conscious or subconscious. Abstract thought is a cold, bare thing, lacking vitality and warmth—desire is filled with life, throbbing, longing, wanting, craving, insisting, and ever pressing forward into action. Desire, indeed, is the motive power of all action. We may call desire by the favorite terms of ambition, aspiration, longing for attainment, etc., but **desire** is ever the basic principle of all longing, all wishing, all wanting.

There have been many attempts to define Desire. Perhaps the best and clearest in its analysis of the essential qualities of Desire is that of Reuben Post Halleck, who has furnished the following definition: **"Desire has for its object something that will bring pleasure or get rid of pain, immediate or remote, for the individual or for someone else in whom he is interested. Aversion, or a striving away from something, is merely the negative aspect of desire."**

Most men act from motives of securing what will bring them the greatest amount of pleasure, or the least amount of pain, immediate or remote, for themselves or for others. In short, men ever strive for **Pleasure** and away from **Pain**.

CHAPTER EIGHT

The Mastery of Desire

The Mastery of Desire does not mean (as some suppose) the "killing out" of all Desire. In fact, as careful students of the subject well know, it would be impossible to kill out all Desire, for the very act of "killing out" would be actually, itself, a response to a desire—a desire not to desire, as it were. Mastery of Desire really means the control, management, and direction of Desire by the Ego.

In beginning the study of the Mastery of Desire, however, we must, of course, begin with the subject of the handling, direction, culture, and control of the Feelings and Emotions, for these are the stuff of which Desire is made. The Ego must learn how to manufacture certain grades and kinds of Feeling and Emotion into Desire, and at the same time to discard and throw into the scrap pile other kinds of Feelings and Emotions, which would make only the wrong kind of Desire.

HOW TO RESTRAIN FEELINGS, EMOTIONS, OR DESIRES

The general rules for the restraint of any class of feelings, emotions, and the desires arising therefrom, are:

I.   Refrain as far as possible from the physical expression of the feeling, or emotion, or the desire arising therefrom, which are deemed objectionable.

II. Refuse to permit the formation of the habit of expressing in action the feeling, or emotion, or the desire arising therefrom, which are deemed objectionable.

III. Refuse to dwell upon the idea or mental picture of the object or subject exciting the feeling, or emotion, or the desire arising therefrom, which are deemed objectionable.

IV. Cultivate the class of feelings or emotions, or the desires arising therefrom, which are opposed to those deemed objectionable.

Let us now consider each one of these rules in further detail:

I. Refrain from the Physical Expression.

A strong feeling or emotion, and the desire arising therefrom, tends toward expression in physical action of some kind. In fact, the feeling is said not to have been fully manifested unless this outward expression is had in at least some degree. This being so, it is seen that if one refrains from the physical expression, he has done something to prevent the full manifestation of the feeling.

So closely are the two—feelings and their physical expression—connected, that some psychologists have actually held that the physical expression precedes and practically causes the mental state of feeling. Some men in important positions make it a rule to maintain an even, low tone of voice when they are threatened with a rush of angry feeling—they have found that such a plan enables them to keep their temper, even under the most trying circumstances. And, in passing, it may be said that such a course will often result in the other person in the quarrel also lowering his voice, and abating his angry feeling.

There is a mutual action and reaction between emotional mental states and the physical expression thereof; each in a measure being the cause of the other, and each at the same time being the effect of the other.

Halleck has noted: "Actors have frequently testified to the fact that emotion will arise if they go through the appropriate muscular movements. In talking to actors on the stage, if they clinch the fists and frown, they often find themselves becoming really angry; if they start with counterfeit laughter, they find themselves growing cheerful . . . If we wish to conquer undesirable emotional tendencies in ourselves, we must assiduously, and in the first instance cold-bloodedly, go through the outward movements of those contrary dispositions which we wish to cultivate. Soothe the brow, brighten the eye, contract the dorsal rather than the ventral aspect of the frame, and speak in a major key, and your heart must be frigid indeed if it does not gradually thaw."

The essence, then, of the above is: **Refrain so far as is possible from indulging in the physical expression of a feeling, emotion, or desire that you wish to conquer, control, and repress.**

II. Refuse to Form the Habit of Expression in Action.

Habits build a mental path over which the Will thereafter travels. Or, to use another figure of speech, Habit cuts a channel, through which the Will afterward flows. When you express a feeling, emotion, or desire in action you begin to form a habit; when you express it the second time the habit takes on force; and so on, each repetition widening the mental path, or deepening the mental channel over which it is easy for subsequent action to travel. The oftener the feeling, emotion, or desire travels this path of action, the stronger it becomes.

The essence of the above is: **Don't get into the habit of expressing in action a feeling, emotion, or desire which you wish to conquer, control, and repress.**

III. Refuse to Dwell upon the Idea or Mental Picture.

This rule is based upon the accepted fact of psychology that Feeling, Emotion, and Desire are fed, nourished, and strengthened by the representative idea, or mental image of the object or subject which has originally inspired them, or which is associated with that object or subject. Feelings are often caused by an idea, resulting from the process of thought or recalled in memory. Likewise they are deepened and strengthened by the recalling into consciousness of such ideas. In the same way, they are fed and nourished by ideas connected with the original object or subject by the ties of association.

The remembrance of an insult, an act of unkindness, a wrong done, may cause acute feeling. There may be no immediately preceding change in the sense organ when an idea flashes into the mind, but the feeling may be just as pronounced as if it were. A **representative**

idea is a revived sensation, or a complex of revived sensations. Some ideas cause a joyful, others a sorrowful mental state; accordingly, feelings differ qualitatively according to the idea. Our feelings also differ quantitatively as the idea has a more or less pleasurable or painful element.

To sum up: Inasmuch as it is a psychological fact that ideas not only cause feelings, emotions, and desires, but also tend to revive, deepen, strengthen, and nourish them, it follows that if one wishes to inhibit, repress, or weaken any disadvantageous feeling, emotion, or desire, he should studiously and insistently refrain from allowing his attention to dwell upon the ideas tending to arouse or stimulate such feelings, emotions, or desires. He should refuse to feed the feeling, emotion, or desire with the nourishing food of associated ideas. Instead, he should set to starve out the objectionable feeling, emotion, or desire by refusing it the mental food needed for its growth.

IV. Cultivate the Opposite.

It is a law of psychology that one set of feelings, emotions, or desires may be weakened, repressed, and controlled by a careful and determined cultivation of the opposite set of feelings, emotions, or desires. Every mental state in the emotional field has its opposite. The two states are antagonistic, and each tends to annihilate the other. The two cannot coexist. One cannot feel happy and miserable at the same time and place. Consequently, there is always a struggle between opposing mental states.

By the *Cultivation of the Opposites*, the person takes advantage of the fight already under way between the two opposing emotional armies, and instead of fighting the battle all alone by a frontal attack, he forms an alliance with the friendly army, and throws the weight of his own will in its favor—he brings up a powerful reserve force, with men, equipment, ammunition, and supplies, and thus gives to the friendly army an enormously increased advantage. One has but to consider the matter in this light in order to see that this is **the best, easiest, and quickest way** to conquer the objectionable mental army.

The above statement is based upon the acknowledged psychological fact expressed in the axiom that: **"To develop a positive quality, it is important to restrain or inhibit its opposing negative; to restrain or inhibit a negative quality, develop and encourage its opposing positive."** In this axiom is condensed a whole philosophy of character-building and self-improvement.

It is equally important to cultivate positive or desired emotions. Here are the general rules for the Cultivation, Development, and Strengthening of *Desirable* Feelings, Emotions, and Desires:

   I. Frequently express, mentally and physically, the feeling, emotion, or desire that you wish to cultivate, develop, and strengthen.

  II. Form the habit of expressing in action the feeling, emotion, or desire that you wish to cultivate, develop, or strengthen.

 III. Keep before you as much as possible the idea or mental image associated with the feeling, emotion, or desire which you wish to cultivate, develop or strengthen.

 IV. Restrain the classes of feelings, emotions, and desires opposed to those you wish to cultivate, develop, or strengthen.

Let us now consider each one of these rules in further detail.

I. Frequently express the positive feelings, emotions, and desires.

As we have seen, a feeling, emotion, or desire is developed by the physical expression thereof, and also by the frequent repetition of the same in consciousness. The expression of the outward physical manifestations of the inner state tends not only to add fuel to the fire of the latter, but also nourishes and strengthens it. Likewise, the frequent bringing into the field of consciousness of the feeling, emotion, or desire tends to deepen the impression, and to cause the mental state to take deep roots in the mental being of the individual.

Exercise and practice develops the emotional muscles, just as they do the physical muscles. Repetition is a potent factor in forming and strengthening mental impressions, and in the cultivation of the mental habits. Consequently, lose no opportunity for exercising and using the feeling, emotion, or desire that you wish to cultivate and develop. If you wish to be courageous, bring up often the idea of courage, and endeavor to feel its thrill through you; and at the same time, deliberately assume the physical attitude of courage. Think of yourself as the courageous individual, and try to walk, carry yourself, and in general act like that individual. Form the correct mental picture, and then endeavor to **act it out.**

Get control of your physical channels of expression, and master the physical expression connected with the mental state you are trying to develop. For instance, if you are trying to develop your will along the lines of Self-Reliance, Confidence, Fearlessness, etc., the first thing for you to do is to get a perfect control of the muscles by which the physical manifestations or expressions of those feelings are shown. Get control of the muscles of your shoulders, that you may throw them back manfully. Look out for the stooping attitude of lack of confidence. Then get control of the muscles by which you hold up your head, with eyes front, gazing the world fearlessly in the face. Get control of your vocal organs, by which you may speak in the resonant, vibrant tones that compel attention and inspire respect.

You must learn to occasionally actually perform some act requiring physical or moral courage. You must exercise your mental state and will by actual use. Grow by expression and action. Do the deeds, and you will acquire the power to do still greater.

The essence, then, of the above is: **Express frequently, mentally and physically, in "acting out" and actual doing, the feeling, emotion, and desire which you wish to cultivate and develop.**

II. Acquire the Habit of Expression.

By acquiring the Habit of Expression of the feeling, emotion, or desire which you may wish to cultivate and develop, you make a mental path or channel over which the will will naturally and easily travel. Habit renders the expression second nature. Habit is formed by exercise and repetition. Every time you express a mental state, the easier it becomes to express it again, for you have started the formation of a habit. Habit is a form of mental impression, and the oftener you sink the die of action into the soft wax of the mind, the deeper will be the impression. Habit increases ease of performance. When a habit is built, it constitutes the line of least resistance, and you will find it easy to move in that direction, and hard to move in the opposite.

Here you must fight with all your might, but, the first battle once won, the after-fights are less severe, and finally degenerate into mere skirmishes.

The essence, of the above is: **Establish firmly the habit of expressing in action the feeling, emotion, or desire that you wish to cultivate.**

III. Visualize the Associated Subject or Object.

It is an established principle of psychology that the mental picture of the object or subject of a feeling, emotion, or desire, when held before the mind, tends to add force, power, and vitality to the emotional state representing it. And the stronger, deeper, clearer, and more frequently repeated such a mental picture is, the stronger, deeper, and more does the emotional mental state associated with it become. Feelings, emotions, and desires are fed by **ideas**—and the strongest kinds of ideas are those taking form in clear mental pictures of the imagination or memory.

The essence, of the above is: **Feed your mind with the ideas and mental pictures of the object or subject of the feeling, emotion, or desire you wish to develop.**

IV. Restrain and Suppress the Opposites.

As we have seen, the development of an opposite set of feelings, emotions, or desires tends to restrain, suppress, and eventually destroy any particular set of these mental states. Contrariwise, it follows that if we will studiously and determinedly restrain and suppress (by the methods already given) the feelings, emotions, and desires opposed to those we wish to cultivate, then will the favored ones be given the best possible opportunity to nourish, grow, develop, and wax strong. Regard the opposing set as **weeds**, which if allowed to grow will choke and weaken, or possibly even kill, your favorite valuable plants. And you know what you should do in such a case, of course: determinedly **weed out** the harmful growths—pluck them by the roots and cast them out of your mental garden the moment they appear.

By refusing to permit the growth of the objectionable emotional weeds of the "opposites" in your mental garden, you greatly promote the growth of the valuable plants. Remember, there is not room in the mental garden for both of the two opposing sets of emotional qualities to thrive. It is up to you to determine which ones shall be the victors— which ones shall be the fittest to survive. The fittest in such cases is not always the **best**—rather is the one that you strengthen, stimulate, and feed. Will you bear a crop of sturdy, strong and vigorous plants and fruits, which are conducive to your wellbeing, strength, efficiency, and ultimate happiness? It is up to you to **decide**—and then to **act.**

CHAPTER NINE

The Mastery of Thought

Speaking in the figurative sense, it may be said that the Kingdom of Mind over which the Ego—or Master Mind—rules (or may rule if it will assert its right and power to rule) is composed of three grand divisions, or states: (1) Feeling; (2) Thought; and (3) Will. The activities of the mind consist of Feeling, Thinking, and Willing. All mental states or processes will be found to come under one or the other of the said classes. And yet, the mental activities are so complex that each of these three respective classes are usually found manifesting in connection with one or more of the others.

We seldom find a Thought without also finding a blending of Feelings, and usually a manifestation of Will, as well. Likewise, we seldom find a Feeling without a Thought connected or associated with it, and usually a manifestation of the presence of Will in connection with it. And, finally, we seldom find a manifestation of Will without the presence of Feeling, and of the Thought associated with the Feeling. But, nevertheless, there is a clear distinction among these three great classes of mental states or processes.

To begin with, let us ask, "What is thought?"

Halleck states: "To think is to compare things with each other, to notice wherein they agree and differ, and to classify them according to these agreements and differences. It enables us to put into a few classes the billions of things that strike our perceptive faculties; to the things with like qualities into a bundle by themselves, and to infer that what is true of one of these things will be true of the others, without actual experience in each individual case; and to introduce law and order into what at first seemed a mass of chaotic materials."

Man has one resource denied to the animals—**the power of progressive thought.** He has harnessed the forces of Nature, proceeding from the grosser to the finer—from steam to electricity—and still has a far more wonderful field to explore.

Many people believe they are "thinking" when they are but exercising their faculty of memory, and even that in merely an idle and passive manner. They are simply allowing the stream of memory to flow through their field of consciousness, while the Ego stands on the banks and idly watches the passing waters of memory flow by. They call this "thinking," while in reality there is no process of Thought under way.

Henry Hazlitt writes: "When I use the word 'thinking,' I mean thinking with a purpose, with an end in view, thinking to solve a problem. I mean the kind of thinking that is forced on us when we are deciding on a course to pursue, on a life work you take up perhaps: the kind of thinking that was forced upon us in our younger days when we had to find a solution to a problem in mathematics . . . I do not mean 'thinking' in snatches, or holding petty opinions on this subject and on that. I mean thought on significant questions which lie outside the bounds of your narrow personal welfare."

The same writer has said: "**If a man were to know everything, he could not think.** Nothing would ever puzzle him, his purposes would never be thwarted, he would never experience perplexity or doubt, he would have no problems . . . If our lives and the lives of our ancestors had always run smoothly, if our every desire were immediately satisfied, if we never met an obstacle in anything we tried to do, thinking would never have appeared on this planet. But adversity forced us to it."

Real thinking is a process directly under the control, direction, and management of the Master Mind. The importance of this fact can be correctly estimated only when one realizes the all-important part played by Thought in the life and welfare of the individual. We are the result of what we have thought. The Master Mind thinks what it wills to think, not what others will it to think, or what Chance determines it shall think. Thus is the Master Mind the Master of Itself.

Chapter Ten

Subconscious Mentality

A large share of the mental processes of the individual play out on some fields or on planes of mentality under or above the ordinary plane of consciousness.

The so-called subconscious or unconscious planes of mind **are not unconscious**, but are really conscious in various degrees of consciousness peculiar to themselves. The term "subconscious" is used simply to indicate that the processes and activities of these particular planes of mind are outside of the field of the ordinary consciousness. When I speak of the passing of impressions, ideas, or records in and out of consciousness, I am not trying to convey the idea of passing these mental images from one mind to another, but rather of passing them in and out of the narrow field of the ordinary consciousness, just as the tiny living creatures in a drop of stagnant water under a microscope pass in and out of the field of vision of the apparatus; or as the stars pass in and out of the field of a stationery telescope as the earth revolves.

Mental events imperceptible to consciousness are far more numerous than the others, and we perceive only the highest points of the world that makes up our being—the lighted-up peaks of a continent whose lower levels remain in the shade. Examine closely, and without bias, the ordinary mental operations of daily life, and you will discover that consciousness has not one-tenth the functions we commonly ascribe to it. In every conscious state there are conscious, subconscious, and infra-conscious energies, each one indispensable.

It must not be supposed that the mind is at any time conscious of all its materials and powers. At any moment we are not conscious of a thousandth part of what we know. It is well that such is the case; for when we are studying a subject, or an object, we should not want all we know to rush into our minds at once. If this occurred, our mental confusion would be indescribable. Between the perception and the recall, the treasures of memory are, metaphorically speaking, away from the eye of consciousness. How these facts are preserved, before they are summoned by memory, consciousness can never tell us. An event may not be thought of for fifty years, and then it may suddenly appear in consciousness.

THE PROCESSES OF IMAGINATION

Imagination, the second class of the processes of the Subconscious Mentality, very closely resembles its brother, the Memory, but there is an important distinction between the two, as follows: Memory reproduces only the original impressions placed within its realm, while Imagination reproduces the recorded impressions of Memory, not in their original condition, but in new groupings, arrangements, and forms.

Memory is the storehouse of impressions, but Imagination is the artist working with these stored up impressions, and making new and wonderful things with them. Imagination takes these stored-away impressions, and **creates** new forms of things from them, but always uses the materials it finds in the Memory storehouse—it makes new combinations, new arrangements, new forms, **but it never makes new materials**.

Imagination is subject to misuse, as well—in fact, the word is frequently employed to indicate the misuse of it, in the form of idle daydreams and vain fanciful flights of the imagination. This misuse arises from the **involuntary** exercise of the Imagination—allowing this subconscious faculty to indulge in purposeless and useless activity. This is like mere daydreaming, and is a habit that often obtains quite a hold over a person if too freely indulged in. It is a mild form of mental intoxication, and the effects are undesirable, for they often manifest in a weakening of the will, and rendering infirm the voluntary purposive faculties of the mind.

The most harmful effects of the idle exercise of the imagination is that it usurps the place rightfully belonging to **action**. It is so much easier and more pleasant to dream of accomplishment than to attempt to make them come true in actual life The habitual daydreamer gradually loses the desire to participate in the activities of life, and slowly sinks into a passive existence.

The best modern psychology recognizes this danger of the misuse of the Imagination, and lays great stress upon the necessity of transmuting the energies of the Imagination into the images of things connected with the life work of the individual, character-building, self-mastery, and general creative work along the lines of the Constructive Imagination. Creative and constructive imagination furnishes the pattern, design, or mold of future action or material manifestation. Properly used, the imagination is the architect of deeds, actions, and accomplishments.

In this constructive and creative work of the Imagination we have but another example of what has been so positively insisted upon: **the principle of the Ego using its instruments of expression, instead of allowing them to use the Ego.** It is the **positive** use of the faculties, instead of the **negative**.

Here follow a few carefully selected rules for the cultivation of the right habits of using the Imagination.

The Supply of Material. Before the Imagination can build, construct, and create, it must be supplied with the proper materials. The materials with which the Imagination works are to be had only in the subconscious storehouse of Memory. Therefore, the Memory must be supplied with a stock of information concerning the particular subject or object. The impressions stored away should be clear, distinct, and strong.

Develop by Exercise. The Imagination should be developed, cultivated, and strengthened by voluntary and directed exercise and use. Acquire the habit of mapping out the work you have to do in advance, and allowing the creative Imagination to fill in the details of the map after you have made the general outlines. Turn your attention upon the tasks before you, and you will discover, providing you have the strong desire for improvement, that the Imagination will set to work suggesting improvements.

Avoid Idle Daydreaming. Avoid the habit of idle daydreaming, for this only dissipates and wastes the energies of the Imagination. Instead, strive to acquire the habit of the purposeful, voluntary use of the Imagination.

Hold to the Central Idea. In the work of Constructive Imagination, always hold firmly to the central idea and purpose of your thought. Build up, tear down, alter, and change the details as much as you see fit, but always with the idea of improving and creating—never allow yourself to be sidetracked. Allow the central idea and its purpose to be the framework upon which you build.

Discard Useless Material. Acquire the habit of discarding all ideas and mental images that are not conducive to your creative work. Hold your mind one-pointed while engaged in your imaginative work. Subject all your ideas and mental images to the test: "Is this conducive to the task in view? Does this tend to efficiency?"

See the Result as You Desire It to Be. Always hold before your mental eye the picture of yourself accomplishing the thing you have set out to do, and picture the result taking on proper form and power.

Describing a scene from his novel *Dr. Jekyll and Mr. Hyde*, author Robert Louis Stevenson offered this portrait of his subconscious and imaginative faculties: "My Brownies! God bless them! who do one-half of my work for me when I am fast asleep, and in all human likelihood do the rest for me as well when I am wide awake and foolishly suppose that I do it for myself. I had long been wanting to write a book on man's double being. For two days I went about racking my brains for a plot of any sort, and on the second night I dreamt the scene in *Dr. Jekyll and Mr. Hyde* at the window; and a scene, afterward split in two, in which Hyde, pursued, took the powder and underwent the change in the presence of his pursuer."

Many pages could be filled with similar testimony to the reality of the processes of Subconscious Thought, to which has been given the names "automatic thinking," "unconscious rumination," or even the picturesque term "the helpful Brownies" of Stevenson.

In the Inner Consciousness of each of us there are forces that act much the same as would countless tiny mental brownies or helpers who are eager to assist us in our mental work, if we will have confidence and trust in them. This is a psychological truth expressed in the terms of the old fairytales. The process of summoning these Inner Consciousness helpers is similar to that we constantly employ to recall some forgotten fact or name. We find that we cannot recollect a desired fact, date, or name, and instead of racking our brains with an increased effort, we (if we have learned the secret) pass on the matter to the Inner Consciousness with a silent command, "Recollect this name for me," and then continue with our ordinary work. After a few minutes—or it may be hours—all of a sudden, pop! will appear the missing name or fact—flashed from the planes of the Inner Consciousness by the help of the kindly workers or "brownies" of those planes. The experience is so common that we have ceased to marvel at it, and yet it is a wonderful manifestation of the Inner Consciousness workings of the mind.

Furthermore, if you will look carefully into a subject you wish to master, and will pass along the results of your observations to these Subconscious Brownies, you will find that they will work the raw materials of thought into shape for you in a comparatively short time. They will arrange, analyze, systematize, collate, and arrange in consecutive order the various details of information that you have passed on to them, and will add articles of similar information that they will find stored away in the various recesses of your memory. In this way, they will group together scattered bits of knowledge that you have forgotten.

There are many ways of setting the brownies to work. Perhaps the best way for the average person is for one to get a very clear idea of what one really wants to know—a clear idea or mental image of the question you wish answered. Then after rolling it around in your mind—mentally chewing it, as it were—giving it a high degree of voluntary attention, you can pass it on to your Subconscious Mentality with the mental command: **"Attend to this for me—work out the answer!"** or some similar order. This command may be given silently, or else spoken aloud—either will do. Speak to the Subconscious Mentality—or its little workers—just as you would speak to people in your employ, kindly but firmly. Talk to the little workers, and command them to do your work. And then forget all about the matter—throw it off your conscious mind, and attend to other tasks. In due time will come your answer—flashed into your consciousness—perhaps not until the very minute that you must decide upon the matter, or need the information. You may give your brownies orders to report at such and such a time—just as you do when you tell them to awaken you at a certain time in the morning, or just as they remind you of the hour of your appointment, if you have them well trained.

The above instruction, though conveyed in a fanciful style, really contains the essence and substance of the most approved methods of making use of the faculties of the subconscious mentality. The reader should carefully study this method, and begin to practice it as he wishes to make use of this wonderful power of the mind. He will find that after a little practice his mental powers will be enormously increased, and his general efficiency added to.

Chapter Eleven

The Mastery of Will

The modern conception of the Will is that of **mental states concerned with action**, the other phases being regarded as subordinate to this.

The Will may be said to present three general phases: (1) The phase in which Desire is being transformed into Will; (2) the phase in which there is the process of Deliberation concerning the respective values of several desires, or several courses of action represented by their respective ideas or mental images; this phase of Deliberation begins with conflicting motives, and ends with a Decision or Choice; (3) the phase of action resulting from the Decision or Choice. The following somewhat fuller statement of each of these phases will aid the reader in perceiving the special characteristics of each.

1. Desire-Will.

All activities of the Will are preceded by Desire. One may Desire without actually setting the Will into operation, but one can scarcely be thought of as Willing without having first experienced the Desire to Will (it being, of course, understood that such Desire may have manifested subconsciously rather than in the conscious field). It is almost impossible to conceive of one willing to do a thing other than from the motive of Desire, either in the form of "wanting to" on the one hand, or of fear on the other hand. Will is always the active expression of some form of Desire.

2. Deliberative Will.

In this second phase of Will activity, there is **a balancing and weighing of desires, or at least a weighing and balancing of several courses of action, in order to determine their values as a channel of expression of the strongest desires.**

Sometimes there is a dominant desire that presses aside all other desires, and asserts its strength and power; in such a case, the deliberation is simply that of determining the best possible channel of expression. But, as a rule, there is first a conflict of desires, which results either in the victory of **the strongest desire present at**

that moment, or else **an average struck between several strong desires then present.**

3. ACTION-WILL.

Some persons can never seem to understand that **resolving** to do a thing is not the same as doing it. Such are utterly worthless in this world of action. They **talk**; they **feel**; they do anything **but act**. They appear to derive almost as much comfort from resolving to answer a letter, which should have been answered two months earlier, as they would from actually writing the reply. There may be desire, deliberation, and decision; but if these do not result in action, the process of will is practically incomplete.

TRAINING THE WILL

Just as the Master Mind may train the faculties of Thought, Feeling, and Emotion, so may it train, control, direct, and master the faculties of the Will. And this last is perhaps the most important of all the various forms of mastery manifested by the Ego, or Master Mind, because the Will is the instrument the Ego uses to control the other mental faculties—and control of the Will is control of the entire situation.

The following Rules of Will Development provide a simple, practical system of training and cultivating the Will.

1. Finding the Center of Power.

This rule consists of bidding the student to find the center of his mental being—the place where dwells the Ego, the Master of Mind, the "I." This involves not only assenting to the presence of the Ego on the part of the intellect, but also of the conscious **feeling** of the presence, reality and power of the **"I"** in the center of the mental field, where it masters, directs, controls, and manages the feelings, emotions, thought processes, objects of attention and desire, and, finally, of the **activities of the will**.

The Ego must learn to turn its attention inward upon itself, and to be conscious of its own presence and existence. It must inwardly cognize itself as the "I"—an actual living entity or being. To do this fully, the Ego must for the moment separate itself from the various instruments and faculties belonging to it—it must see and feel itself simply as the pure Ego—the "I AM!" Each time you control or direct the mind, say to yourself "**I**, the Ego, the Master Mind, am doing this"—and you will be made conscious of a dawning realization of the Ego, which is Yourself—your **Real Self**.

2. Exert Your Will Power.

Exert Your Will Power by practicing the control over the several mental and emotional faculties: **Will** to think; **Will** to **feel**; **Will** to **act**. For instance, you may feel a desire to do, or not do a certain thing—here is your chance to prove your Willpower. Deliberately determine that you **shall and will** desire and feel the exact opposite of your present desire, and then proceed to manifest in action that idea and determination. You will find that the original desire or feeling will struggle and rebel—it will fight hard for life and power—but you must oppose it to the deadly cold steel of your will, as directed by the Master Mind. Persevere, and yield not an inch—assert your mastery of your mental domain. Ask no quarter, and give none; and as sure as tomorrow's sun will rise, so surely will your will triumph. For the Will is positive to other mental states, when it is properly applied and persistently exerted.

3. Consider Your Actions.

Cultivate the faculty of careful deliberation and intelligent determination. In short, look before you leap. Test your feelings, emotions, impulses, and desires by the light of intellect. Test every desire and impulse by the Touchstone of Positivity: "Will this make me stronger, better, and more efficient?" Do not prolong your deliberation too long, however—learn to decide carefully but at the same time quickly and without dawdling. **Then,** when you have determined upon your course of

action—have decided **what** to do, and **how** to do it, as
well as understanding **why** you should do it—proceed
to **actually do it with all your might**. Follow the old
maxim: "Be sure you're right, then go ahead!"

4. Cultivate the Attention.

Carefully cultivate the Attention until you can focus it
upon any object or subject with concentrated force and
insistent direction. The Attention determines the path
of the will—either toward or away from the object of
the Attention. Attention is the eye of the Ego, or Master
Mind, the driver of the mental chariot.

5. Acquire the Habit of Mastery.

Carefully cultivate and acquire the habit of controlling
your mental faculties, feelings, desires, and thoughts,
as well as your actions, by the power of your awakened
will. When you have acquired this habit, half the battle is over. Then will the wild horses of the mind have
learned the lesson of control, and will interpose a constantly decreasing degree of resistance, and a constantly
increasing obedience.

6. Occasionally Perform Disagreeable Tasks.

You will find that it is of great benefit to occasionally
drive your mental steeds in directions contrary to that

which they wish to travel. This course is advisable, not because the agreeable way is necessarily wrong, but simply because such exercise of control trains them and accustoms them to the direction of the Master Mind.

One writer mentions the case of a man who was found reading a particularly dry work on political economy. His friend expressed surprise at his choice of a book, and the man replied: **"I am doing this because I dislike it!"** He was training his mental horses. One of the best and simplest methods of putting this rule into practice is that of heeding the popular adage: "DO IT NOW!" Procrastination is a particularly balky horse, and one that requires careful and persistent attention.

THE "JAMES FORMULAS"

No presentation of the best modern thought concerning the Cultivation of Willpower would be complete without mentioning the celebrated formulas of the great American psychologist William James. Professor James based these formulas upon those of philosopher Alexander Bain, elaborating the latter and adding some equally good advice to them. Here is a condensed statement of the "James Formulas."

1. "In the acquisition of a new habit, or the leaving off of an old one, launch yourself with as strong

and decided an initiative as possible. This will give your new beginning such a momentum that the temptation to break down will not occur as soon as it otherwise might; and every day during which a breakdown is postponed adds to the chances of it not occurring at all."

2. "Never suffer an exception to occur till the new habit is securely rooted in your life. Every lapse is like the letting fall of a ball of string which one is carefully winding up—a single slip undoes more than a great many turns will wind again." "It is necessary, above all things, in such a situation, never to lose a battle. Every gain on the wrong side undoes the effect of many conquests on the right. The essential precaution is so to regulate the two opposing powers that the one may have a series of uninterrupted successes, until repetition has fortified it to such a degree as to enable it to cope with the opposition, under any circumstances."

3. "Seize the very first possible opportunity to act on every resolution you make, and on every emotional prompting you may experience in the direction of the habits you wish to gain. It is not the moment of their forming, but in the moment of their producing motor effects, that resolves, and aspirations communicate their new 'set' to the brain.

The actual presence of the practical opportunity alone furnishes the fulcrum upon which the lever can rest, by which the moral will may multiply its strength and raise itself aloft. He who has no solid ground to press against will never get beyond the stage of empty gesture making."

4. "Keep the faculty alive in you by a little gratuitous exercise every day. That is, be systematically ascetic or heroic in little, unnecessary points; do every day something for no other reason than that you would rather not do it, so that when the hour of dire need draws nigh, it may find you not unnerved and untrained to stand the test. The man who has daily inured himself to habits of concentrated attention, energetic volition, and self-denial in unnecessary things will stand like a tower when everything rocks around him, and when his softer mortals are winnowed like chaff in the blast."

In closing, the student who is striving to develop his Willpower will do well to hold before his mental vision the Inspiring Ideal of the Goal toward which he is struggling and striving.

Benjamin Disraeli wrote: "I have brought myself by long meditation to the conviction that a human being with a settled purpose must accomplish it, and that nothing can resist a will which will stake even existence upon its fulfillment."

Decide which you wish to be: Master Mind or Slave Mind. You have the choice— make it! I have led you to the spring from which bubbles the Waters of Mastery—but I cannot force you to drink. In the words of an old writer: "Man must be either the Anvil or the Hammer—let each make his choice, and then complain not."

"Theron Q. Dumont" was one of several pseudonyms used by WILLIAM WALKER ATKINSON, a popular and innovative New Thought writer and publisher in the early twentieth century. Born in Baltimore, Maryland, in 1862, Atkinson became a successful attorney in 1894. Following a series of illnesses, he immersed himself in New Thought literature. He soon became an important figure in the early days of the movement, publishing magazines such as *Suggestion, New Thought*, and *Advanced Thought*. Under the aegis of his own publishing company, Yogi Publication Society, Atkinson wrote many self-bylined works, and many titles under the pseudonyms Yogi Ramacharaka, Magus Incognito, Theron Q. Dumont, and Three Initiates. Under the last of these, Atkinson wrote his most popular and enduring work, *The Kybalion*. Published in 1908 by Atkinson's Chicago-based press, *The Kybalion* is perhaps the most widely read occult book of the twentieth century. Atkinson died in California in 1932.

MITCH HOROWITZ, who abridged and introduced this volume, is the PEN Award-winning author of books including *Occult America* and *The Miracle Club: How Thoughts Become Reality*. *The Washington Post* says Mitch "treats esoteric ideas and movements with an even-handed intellectual studiousness that is too often lost in today's raised-voice discussions." Follow him @MitchHorowitz.